If you were a

Preposition

RIVERDALE PUBLIC LIBRARY DISTRICT

by Nancy Loewen
(illustrated by Sara Gray)

under

over

behind

beside

onto

PICTURE WINDOW BOOKS
Minneapolis, Minnesota

preposition (prep) a word that shows the relation between another word and a noun or pronoun

Editor: Christianne Jones
Designer: Tracy Kaehler
Page Production: Lori Bye
Creative Director: Keith Griffin
Editorial Director: Carol Jones
The illustrations in this book were
created with acrylics.

Picture Window Books
5115 Excelsior Boulevard
Suite 232
Minneapolis, MN 55416
877-845-8392
www.picturewindowbooks.com

Printed in the United States of America.

**Library of Congress
Cataloging-in-Publication Data**
Loewen, Nancy, 1964–
If you were a preposition / by Nancy Loewen ;
illustrated by Sara Gray.
p. cm. — (Word fun)
Includes bibliographical references.
ISBN-13: 978-1-4048-2386-0 (hardcover)
ISBN-10: 1-4048-2386-7 (hardcover)
ISBN-13: 978-1-4048-2390-7 (paperback)
ISBN-10: 1-4048-2390-5 (paperback)
1. English language—Prepositions—Juvenile literature.
I. Gray, Sara, ill. II. Title. III. Series.
PE1335.L64 2006
428.2—dc22   2006003395

Looking for prepositions?

Watch for the big, colorful words in the example sentences.

Special thanks to our advisers for their expertise:

Rosemary G. Palmer, Ph.D., Department of Literacy
College of Education, Boise State University

Susan Kesselring, M.A., Literacy Educator
Rosemount—Apple Valley—Eagan (Minnesota) School District

If you were a preposition ...

3

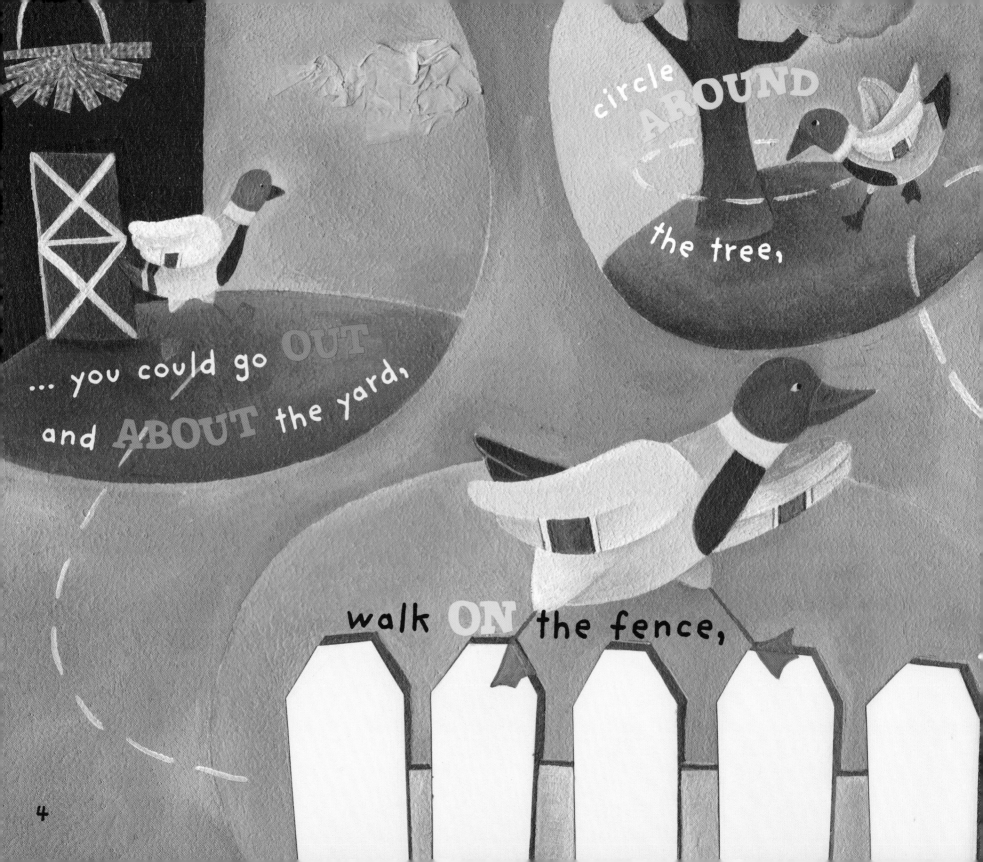

circle AROUND the tree,

... you could go OUT and ABOUT the yard,

walk ON the fence,

4

slither **BETWEEN** the bushes,

or jog **BY** the snail.

If you were a preposition, you would make a sentence longer by adding more detail.

The rabbit hid **INSIDE** the hat.

I want the lizard **WITH**
the red stripes.

If you were a preposition, you could tell where things are.

The goat is walking BESIDE the shed.

The goat
is resting
BEHIND
the shed.

Look! The goat jumped ONTO the shed.

9

If you were a preposition, you could tell when things happen.

DURING the day, Hammy the hamster sleeps.

Hammy drinks his water BEFORE he works out.

10

Hammy runs on his wheel **AT** night.

11

If you were a preposition, you would never work alone. You would be paired with a noun or pronoun. The noun or pronoun would be your object. You and your object would form a prepositional phrase.

prepositional phrase

Tibby ate two whole cans **OF tuna!**

(preposition)　(object)

12

All three cats sleep **WITH me**.
(prep.) (obj.)

Here, kitty!
Come **TO me**.
(prep.) (obj.)

13

If you were a preposition, you could be part of a short prepositional phrase.

prepositional phrase

ON Wednesday
(prep.)   (obj.)

prepositional phrase

TOWARD her
(prep.)   (obj.)

If you were a preposition, you could be part of a prepositional phrase that includes many words. These words are called modifiers. They describe people, places, things, or actions. Modifiers go between the preposition and the object of the preposition.

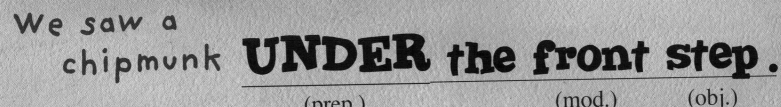

We saw a chipmunk **UNDER** the front step.
(prep.)   (mod.)   (obj.)

16

The dog fell asleep
BY the warm, cozy fireplace.
(prep.) (mod.) (mod.) (obj.)

17

If you were a preposition, you could be in a sentence with other prepositional phrases.

The tarantula crawled FROM its cage,

OVER the stack
OF books,

ACROSS the desk,

and INTO the

wastebasket.

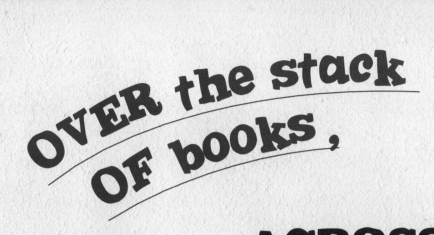

If you were a preposition, you could make a sentence more exciting. The sentence would make sense without you, but it wouldn't be nearly as much fun.

The ferret jumped.

The ferret jumped
FROM the table,
TO the lamp, and
ONTO the drapes.

You would link words together
and add more detail ...
... if you were a preposition!

Position your Prepositions

With a group of friends, write down as many prepositions as you can. Cut the words apart, and put them in a bowl. Take turns drawing a word and acting it out. Look around for objects you can use to demonstrate the word.

For example, if you get the word "through," you could pass a coin through the slats of a kitchen chair. The first person to guess the correct answer gets a point.

Some of the prepositions will be easy to act out. Others will be difficult. You may want to give each player a hint, like what letter the preposition starts with. You could also think of a sentence using the preposition, and then say the sentence out loud without using the preposition.

Once all of the words are drawn, the person with the most points wins.

Fact: If you look up a preposition in the dictionary, you will see the abbreviation "prep" next to it. The "prep" stands for preposition.

Glossary

modifiers—words that go between the preposition and the object of the preposition and describe people, places, things, or actions

noun—a word that names a person, place, or thing

object—a noun or pronoun that ends a phrase that begins with a preposition

phrase—a group of words that expresses a thought but is not a complete sentence

preposition—a word that shows the relation between another word and a noun or pronoun

prepositional phrase—a phrase that begins with a preposition and ends with an object

pronoun—a word that takes the place of a noun

To Learn More

At the Library

Cleary, Brian P. *Under, Over, By the Clover: What Is a Preposition?* Minneapolis: Carolrhoda Books, 2002.

Heinrichs, Ann. *Prepositions.* Chanhassen, Minn.: Child's World, 2004.

Heller, Ruth. *Behind the Mask: A Book About Prepositions.* New York: Grosset & Dunlap, 1995.

On the Web

FactHound offers a safe, fun way to find Internet sites related to this book. All of the sites on FactHound have been researched by our staff.

1. Visit *www.facthound.com*
2. Type in this special code for age-appropriate sites: 1404823867
3. Click on the FETCH IT button.

Your trusty FactHound will fetch the best sites for you!

Look for all of the books in the Word Fun series:

If You Were a Conjunction	1-4048-2385-9
If You Were a Noun	1-4048-1355-1
If You Were a Preposition	1-4048-2386-7
If You Were a Pronoun	1-4048-2637-8
If You Were a Verb	1-4048-1354-3
If You Were an Adjective	1-4048-1356-X
If You Were an Adverb	1-4048-1357-8
If You Were an Interjection	1-4048-2636-X